For information on bulk sales, call 814.218.0563 or email

info@buyingfirsthomes.com.

First published in 2019.

"Real estate cannot be lost or stolen, nor can it be carried away. Purchased with common sense, paid for in full, and managed with reasonable care, it is about the safest investment in the world."

-Franklin D. Roosevelt

Preface

Many years ago (and well before going into the real estate business), I went on, what I thought was going to be, a great adventure… I had decided to buy my first home. I was excited to look at houses and find that perfect place to make my home. I watched those shows where the buyers look at three homes that the rest of us cannot afford, choose one, and, poof, their offer is accepted. This excitement quickly faded to frustration and stress when I came to the realization that what I liked, I couldn't afford, and, what I could afford, I simply didn't like. After 18 months, 12 rejected offers, and, God only knows how many dozens and dozens of homes I walked through, I finally found the right house at the right price. The moral of this story is that I, like many other first-time homebuyers, went into the process uneducated. I sauntered into the market with a childlike naiveté. I lacked the basic understanding of what this endeavor would entail. I fell short of having the knowledge and confidence to truly grasp what I was looking for within my budget, how to construct a worthy offer, what to expect throughout the process, and what professionals I should seek to streamline this endeavor.

In American culture, homeownership has always been regarded as a cornerstone of the evolution into adulthood and a benchmark of personal success. Most first time home buyers (including myself), enter into the market with the dream of the cliché describing the house with a yard and a white picket fence.

This process is and should be a very exciting adventure, that said, for the underinformed buyer, this excitement can quickly fade into a stressful, overwhelming nightmare. The purpose of this prose is to lay a basic foundation of knowledge as to the homebuying process. It is part of the excitement, and a responsibility solely up to you, to build upon this foundation and assure yourself that you possess the necessary knowledge to make an informed purchase and accept all the duties that go along with owning a home.

As the late, great FDR pointed out above, owning a home can be a very safe investment into the security of you and your family, but there are many pits you can fall into without taking time to educate yourself as to what you are actually purchasing.

As you turn the pages contained herein, you are taking a large step forward in carrying out your responsibility to be informed. With the conclusion of this script, we will remind you, however, that your job is far from done. Every town, every neighborhood, every street represents an independent and fluidly evolving real estate market in and of itself. It is up to you to seek the necessary insight into these ever-changing markets. As will be explored in greater detail in Chapter Four, consulting with and/or working with a licensed real estate agent is an important consideration to this point.

As I opened above with the story of my first home buying experience, I will offer that the mere fact that you are reading these words has set you eons ahead of me when I set out on my first home buying mission. My co-author and I took a different approach to penning this book. I, John, wrote the first four chapters, and Melanie wrote chapter five to the end. In addition, we should say that this book is based off of our knowledge and expertise of the northwest Pennsylvania market. While some items contained within these pages can be applied in other cities, other states and other markets, please keep that in mind.

Without further delay, sit back, relax, and continue to turn the pages…
The American Dream awaits!

One

Getting Started: The excitement and the *stress*

On the face of it, the homebuying process is a simple one: you find the home of your dreams, sign on the dotted line, keys are slid across the table, you call every friend with a truck and that's it, welcome home! Unfortunately, there is a big difference between the overly simplistic TV portrayal of buying a home and, well, real life. The reality of buying a home in today's market place is far more complicated (but do-able!).

The single most important consideration, no matter if you are a first-time home buyer or a seasoned veteran of home purchasing, is financing.

Let's face it, not many of us (your authors included) are capable of walking into a real estate transaction with the ability to pay for the property in cold hard dead presidents (AKA cash). While this would be a wonderful luxury, it simply isn't a reality for most of us. To this point, financing is critical and should remain at the top of your to-do list from day one. There are many types of financing (as will be explored in greater detail in Chapter Three) and different types of lending institutions, but the net result is still the same: in order to buy anything, and specific to our topic, a home, you need money. This is typically in the form of a mortgage from a bank or other lending institution.

What, exactly, is a mortgage, you ask?

Most home buyers believe that a mortgage simply defined, is a loan for the purchase of real estate. Technically speaking, this is not true. A mortgage is the lender's legal right to foreclose on the property and sell the house should you default on the note, which is the actual loan. Most people equate the mortgage as the loan and use the terms interchangeably, so, for our purposes we will do the same and carry the two terms as synonyms.

As stated above, there are many forms of a mortgage which we will discuss in latter pages, but simply stated, a mortgage is when a bank or other lending institution agrees to pay the seller for a property up front. They assume the risk of whether or not the mortgagor (you) will pay them back. You, in return, agree to pay the lender back on a schedule of payments for the principal (the purchase price of the property) plus interest (added fees which is the lender's profit for assuming the risk of the loan... this is how the lender makes their money). We will also cover interest in greater depth in the pages that follow.

Buyers, START YOUR ENGINES!!

Your first step should be to schedule an appointment with a lender to obtain a pre-approval. A pre-approval is a simple process which generally can be done in person, over the phone, or via the internet and usually is done within minutes.

DISCLAIMER: A pre-approval is **_not_** a mortgage approval.

The pre-approval process considers only a small fraction of the information that will be asked of you to produce during the formal mortgage application process. It is the effective equivalent to applying for a credit card. The mortgage officer will take specific information to view your credit. For our purposes, we will use a very simplistic definition of what credit means. Credit is made up of several components, but, again, for our purposes, we will consider it as constructed by your account payment history coupled with your debt to income ratio (i.e. how much you owe vs. how much you make).

When these are put together it derives what is known as your credit score. The score is a numeric value that lenders rely very heavily on when evaluating the amount of risk you represent as a borrower. A perfect credit score is 850. A score greater than 700 is considered "good". Marginal scores would be in the 600 range and any score that falls below 599 would be considered "poor". Your credit worthiness will have a tremendous impact on whether or not a lender will loan you money and at what interest rate. Generally speaking, the better your credit, the lower the interest rate you receive; the lower the interest rate you receive translates into big savings over the long term.

Another component to your credit score is the amount of available credit you have and the length, in time, that your credit history has existed. This can be a detriment to younger people simply because they have not been on Earth long enough to establish a credit history. An experienced loan officer can assist you with credit woes, however.

Now that we understand credit, back to your all-important pre-approval process. To begin this endeavor, pick a lender, any lender. Most people utilize the bank where they have a pre-existing account for either a savings or checking account, or an auto loan. You should keep in mind that you are not obligated to use the lender that prepares your pre-approval as your actual mortgage holder. As stated above, the mortgage officer (or website) will ask certain information to complete your application. Within a few minutes you should have your answer, to which, we all hope consists of the word…

"(Pre-)APPROVED"!

Once you are pre-approved, most lenders will give you a ceiling amount in which they have pre-approved you for. Let's use an example: ABC Bank pre-approves you for $250,000. This does *not* necessarily mean that you can, in fact, afford a $250,000 mortgage. What it means is that based on the components that make up your credit, the lender feels comfortable, once several other factors are satisfied, loaning you this amount. We will cover preparing an effective budget in Chapter Two, but this is the preliminary number that sets your upper limit at least preliminarily. You will then be presented with a pre-approval letter. You will want to hang on to this.

CASH Money

Once you have your pre-approval letter, ask the mortgage officer to provide an estimate as to how much cash you will need to complete the purchase. Some lenders will ask how much cash you have as part of the pre-approval process, but some will not unless you bring it up to them. This is a critical detail moving forward. You will need cash for a variety of fees. When your offer is accepted, you will be required to come up with a deposit. This amount varies and is usually relative to the cost of the property. You will also encounter a few "up-front" costs such as home inspections, appraisals, and credit reporting fees that you will be required to pay for at various times during the process. The balance of the monies due would comprise what is called "closing costs" which, as the name implies, you will need at the closing when you actually take possession of the property. We will re-visit this topic again, but the bottom line is you will need money to make the wheels spin.

A Shopping List

At this point, you have your pre-approval in hand and enough cash available to begin looking for a house. It is now time to start deciding what you are actually looking for in the homes you will be looking at. This seems like a common-sense item, but, in our experience, you would be amazed how many people dive head first into the housing market with little-to-no thought as to what they are actually looking to buy.

People would not walk into a clothing store, approach the clerk, and say, "I need you to find me a shirt.", and expect the clerk to produce exactly what they are looking for. There would be several questions to follow, "Short sleeve or long sleeve?", "Casual or dressy?", etc. The housing market is no different.

You need to consider your lifestyle and, relative to it, what you need out of a house aside from a roof and four walls. We recommend that people at this stage sit down and start thinking about what you actually need. This brainstorming should be separated into two categories: *Wants* and *Needs*. From one person to the next, these lists will vary greatly. For instance, if you are young and healthy, you may *want* a ranch (one-story) style house, but it is not critical. Those looking to downsize, folks who are older, or those with physical limitations may absolutely *need* a home where they are not required to climb stairs.

Needs are the most important so they should be considered first. These are absolute must haves, deal breakers. If you are or are planning on being a pet owner, the property would need to be able to accommodate animals. If you have, or are planning on having, children, possessing enough space for the kiddos is important. A particular school district may be important to some, but not to others. There are several variables that go into this thought process so you should take your time and think long term. Most people are going to remain in a home for an extended period of time, years in fact. You need to consider how long you intend to stay in the home and all the life events that could take place during that time. These events will impact your lifestyle and the choices you make on your first home are critical to allow for the lifestyle you seek. For nearly all of us, the purchase of a home is the largest transaction we will ever complete at that point of our lives. You do not want to put yourself in a position that causes regret because you didn't take the time to perform due diligence early on relative to what you truly need. The last thing you want is the necessity to move prematurely because you did not take the time to consider these events as compared to your initial timetable. Long story, short, if you want to stay in your first home for at least five years, think about where life will take you in that time span. Again, everyone's goals will differ here, take your time considering yours.

I want it, I want it…

Wants are important, but not necessarily deal breakers. In this category, you should consider what would be ideal, but not critical. Wants are very relative and individual in nature. For example, you may want to be located close to work. This may seem like an important factor, but at the end of the day, if you find a home that addresses all of your needs and most other wants, would it be a deal breaker to have to add an extra ten minutes to your commute? Only you can define the importance to these items.

The needs vs. wants list will evolve over time especially as you get more educated in the market. Consider a buyer that has "minimum of four bedrooms and located in ABC School District" as two items on their needs list. As they research homes available in this area, they learn that the homes built in this area almost exclusively have 2-3 bedrooms. At this point they would have to make a choice as to what is truly a need and which is a want. This can cause some frustrating moments as you discover that what you want may not be available and can cause for some difficult decisions.   In addition, as we will talk about in Chapter Five, there may be potential in the home when it comes to finishing a basement to make it into an extra room.

These lists will also have to take budget into consideration. The next chapter will address budgeting in greater detail, but this is an important consideration when building your wants/needs lists. A critical perspective to have is that, quite simply, sellers always want the maximum amount of money possible in the sale of a property; conversely, buyers want the best value when purchasing a home. It is unrealistic that you will purchase a palatial estate for the cost of a bungalow. The goal, as a buyer, would be to get the most possible for your money while respecting the seller's financial needs. This can be a difficult balance to achieve and requires some education as to what is realistic within your budget, one of the many reason why it is a major plus to having a licensed real estate agent or Realtor in your corner. They can assist in this education process and expose you to what is available within your established price range. Above all, don't fall into the trap of setting yourself up for disappointment by having overly, unrealistic expectations based on what you can afford.

With all of the above said, remember, this is your first home purchase. While you should never settle on a property just to buy a property, you are probably not going to buy your "forever home" as your first home. You will always be nostalgic towards your first home; no one should suggest otherwise, the point here, though, is to be realistic. When you complete your initial wants/needs list, hang on to it. After the purchase is settled, and you are all moved in, review it compared to your final version and the home that you purchased. It is safe to say that many of your initial "needs" migrated to the "wants" side, if not got crossed off completely. This is normal for nearly all of us. As you receive your market education and realize what you can afford, this evolution as to your list is natural. As a first-time home buyer, I would suggest that you approach as more of a business decision. As stated earlier, consider how long you plan on staying in the house. The average first-time home buyer occupies their first home for 5-7 years. Understanding what your goals are is important. The suggestion here is simple:

- Find a property that hits as many of your needs as possible (and, hopefully, some wants as well)
- **Find a property that fits your budget!** (More on this in Chapter Two)
- Find a property that within your goal timeframe will appreciate in value and allow you to climb the real estate ladder towards the mythical creature known as the "forever home"

Key chapter points:

1. Pre-approval is your number one top priority before looking into the housing market.
2. You will need cash, research how much you will need and make sure that this is attainable.
3. Prepare your needs vs. wants list realistically and allow it to modify itself along the way.

> "A budget is more than just a series of numbers on a page; it is an embodiment of our values."

> -Barack Obama

Two

Dollars and sense: Establishing a budget

Now that you have your preliminary lists prepared and have your all-important pre-approval letter, you are ready to run out and buy a house… NO, we have more work to do. At this point you have perhaps the most important task of the preparation process in front of you, budgeting.

Preparing an accurate personal/household budget can be a challenging endeavor, but the benefits are endless. It can provide for financial accountability and give you greater confidence to know where your money is going. It allows for you to prioritize and manage your debts. It also gives you the freedom to establish that often spoken about, mythical creature known as a savings account. There are libraries of books written about how to accomplish all the above, but, for our purposes, this chapter will spend a few pages talking about the basics of budgeting so that you can strut confidently into the market and prepare

With that pre-approval, the lender will typically tell you a number that they feel comfortable lending you given the information then existing. This does not mean that you can, in reality, afford that amount in the form of a monthly payment. The preparation of a budget gives you the peace of mind that you will not wind up house poor. Because, you know, you may like to occasionally eat as well.

Some of you may be smarter than me at this stage of life, and are already living under a defined, disciplined budget. Others, like me at that time, understand their bills and pay them on time, but do not necessarily keep up to the minute records and have a firm grasp on exactly how much those bills tally up to versus how much they bring in. I would often say to myself at the end of each month (and sometimes each week), "Where did all my money go?".

Regardless of which group you fall into, budgeting, at its essence, is simple. Budgeting is putting on paper what you bring in (income) every month, contrasting that to all of your known money going out (expenses), and setting limits on all of your creature comfort expenditures (we'll call those luxury items). The goal is to define every expenditure and to provide accountability for where you spend your money. This can be done on a bar napkin, a crumpled-up piece of paper, or, for the more tech savvy, a spreadsheet. It can be in crayon, penciled, or in calligraphy, as long as it is done.

The difficulty in budgeting comes in two forms. The first, is the shock factor when we all realize how frivolously we spend our hard-earned pay checks. It can be disconcerting to realize, when you add it all up, how much we actually spend in a month on eating out every day for lunch. The second area where people wind up in the weeds is the discipline that will be required, but we'll talk more about that in just a bit. Let us first discuss the preparation of budget.

On your paper (or bar napkin), start with four columns headed:

1. **INCOME**
2. **BILLS**
3. **LUXURY**
4. **HOUSING**

The easy part for most people is compiling your income. Consider all your income, but keep it realistic. If you are a salaried employee, you should know exactly how much your paycheck is from week to week. If you are salaried, but receive, quarterly bonuses, or you are an hourly employee who gets overtime, budget for the minimum. In other words, budget for what you consider to be guaranteed, anything extra is gravy! This category can be a bit more challenging if your income is commission based (like us hard working real estate agents). Should your paycheck be solely based on commission, be careful. We in the commission only field know that it is feast or famine. The advice here is to, again, be realistic. You would want to stay conservative, but do not sell yourself short. With this number in hand, we get to the second column, the one that everyone hates… bills.

I can confidently say that there is not a person on the planet that likes paying bills, but they are a necessary evil. Take your time. Be honest and thorough in this category. Take that pile of bills and account for each one with their average payment.

This column includes all your regular expenditures. It should encompass such things as car payments, gasoline, cell phone, utilities (more on that in a moment), student loans, insurance, groceries, etc. Also remember to include miscellaneous line item here as well. We all know that there are expenses that creep up on us from the shadows. Whether it be car repairs, medical expenses, speeding tickets (my co-author has a lead foot), etc. be prepared as best you can. This is also a way to build up your savings account by depositing your unused miscellaneously budgeted money.

When it comes to utilities, obviously heating and cooling/electrical expenses are variable based the seasons. A quick call to most energy companies can reveal an average monthly payment over the past year as if you had been paying in this way. If your provider does not supply this, do your best to estimate an accurate monthly budget. The same is true of other variable expenses such as groceries. This figure will fluctuate from time to time, but do your best and again, accuracy and honesty is the key.

As I said before, seeing all your bills on paper can be shocking, but it can also be quite therapeutic. The true soul searching is about to come in your next assignment…

The luxury category is the time where we call ourselves out, so to speak. Now is the time when we think hard and force that dreaded accountability to the forefront. While there may be a hand full of bills we have control over, but most are forced upon us. Luxury items are within our complete and total control. These expenditures are largely lifestyle choices. For example, going out to dinner or drinks, those $4 lattes, clothing, car washes, and so on and so on. I am certainly not claiming that you do not need clothing, or suggesting that going out to dinner or partaking in happy hour are bad things, but we do control how often we buy clothes and eat out and how much we spend when doing so. You may find that you are eating out five times a week and when you question where all your money goes, this would be an easy expense to save in. This accountability can help you immensely in the long term, but for our purposes, let us just consider what you expect to spend in a month on these items. I know I am nagging when I say this again, but *be honest*. Your honesty and attention to detail are perhaps most important in this category.

Now that you have spent some time compiling a thorough and honest list of these items, it is time to consider how much you can afford in housing. A very quick estimate says that most people can pay approximately 25-30% of their gross monthly income towards housing. In any case, it is generally not advisable to extend that figure beyond 30%. When you add all of your projected expenditures from the expenses and luxury columns you then subtract that from your income, that lump sum is your max budget for a mortgage payment. We will discuss in the next chapter the different types of mortgage options and how they affect your monthly payments, but once you have this number, work with your loan officer to establish your true maximum budget for housing.

Key chapter points:

1. Take a deep breath; this will help you over the long run.
2. To establish a personal budget, put a title to every penny you spend.
3. **<u>BE HONEST. BE DISCIPLINED.</u>**

Three

Bonkers for Bankers: The Wild World of Residential Lending

FHA, VA, Conventional, Jumbo, ARM, USDA, HUD, etc., etc., etc.... These are but a handful of residential lending programs available to consumers. This chapter also could be a book in and of itself. There are obviously a multitude of lending opportunities available out there. My task in this chapter is to familiarize you with the most common types of loans available to you. As we spoke about previously, when you get started, one of your first tasks is to speak to a loan officer about your preapproval. At the time of the preapproval, you should be having a conversation with the loan officer about what programs are offered and which ones you would qualify for. From this list, you, with the guidance of your loan officer, can narrow down to what program best fits your needs.

The following pages will go over a few of the more common types of loan programs available to first time buyers. Please understand that this is not an all-inclusive list, nor is it intended to be an "owner's manual" of sorts. These loan programs change frequently and vary by the laws and regulations of where you are obtaining the loan. While you familiarize yourself with the programs available to you, I would implore you to keep open dialogue with your loan officer to learn more about the most important loan most of us will take in our lives.

Conventional Mortgages:

Conventional loans are not as common among first time buyers but are still available so let's chat about them briefly. These types of loans require the buyer to put a down payment equal to a percentage of the purchase price. They generally require higher minimum credit scores and obviously you are required to prove that you have the cash on hand to cover the down payment. The most common conventional loan is a 30 year fixed with a 20% down payment. Whoa, that was a mouthful!! Let's break that down.

30 Years is the term of the loan, or how long you have to pay off the loan. You will pay this in monthly installments on an amortization schedule. An amortization schedule breaks down how your loan payment is dispersed between principal and interest. At the beginning of the loan period, a very small amount of the payment actually goes towards the principal of what you borrowed. Most of the payment will cover interest. This protects the lender as the first few years of a loan are the riskiest for them, as most people who default on loans do so in the first few years. As the years pass, this ratio will swing more so in your favor as you pay off the loan. At closing, one of the documents you'll receive is your amortization schedule. There are other terms available which will pay off the loan sooner, but will, conversely raise your monthly payment. Examples of this would be 10, 15, or sometimes 20-year terms.

Fixed refers to your interest rate. In this case, it means that the interest rate will never change over the life of the loan. Some loan programs offer adjustable rates where your interest rate will change as rates change in the outside financial world. Sometimes adjustable rate loans can be advantageous, but talk this over with your loan officer if this is something you are considering!

20% is the amount you need to put down. For example, to use this type of financing on a $100,000 house, you would need to bring a *cashier's check* (nothing will derail a closing like trying to pay a down payment (not to be confused with an initial deposit) or closing costs with a personal check) in the amount of $20,000… not chump change. Some of our readers will have this kind of cash on hand, but, others may have saved their pennies and are able to put a sizable down payment forward. Another possibility which comes up from time to time is someone, typically a family member, may gift the money to you. In these cases, the lucky recipient will need to provide the lender with what is known as a "gift letter". This assures the lender that the cash involved was legally obtained and is written by the party giving you the money.

The major advantage of a conventional loan is that it eliminates the need for PMI, or **P**rivate **M**ortgage **I**nsurance. PMI is an insurance taken out by the lender to protect against you, the borrower, defaulting on your loan. We will delve more into this more in this chapter, but the take away is that if you have the financial ability to enter into a conventional mortgage; it can certainly save you some money!

FHA Mortgages:

FHA stands for **F**ederal **H**ousing **A**dministration loans. These loan programs are federally backed loan programs primarily intended to assist with home buyers that lack the upfront cash to secure a conventional loan. It operates very similarly to VA loans which we will discuss next. The vast majority of first-time home buyers will be using either FHA or VA loan programs. The beauty of the FHA program is that it requires far less down than its conventional counterpart. The typical FHA program only requires 3.5% down. For example, on a $100,000 purchase, conventional loans require you to have at least $20,000 in the bank. FHA would only require $3,500 on hand (plus those pesky closing costs). "This is spectacular!", you say, and while it is a great program for many buyers, you should (and need to) understand the fine print. FHA is strict with their regulations as they are ensuring the lenders that you will pay your loan back.

They will require an inspection which coincides with the appraisal (don't worry, we will explain what appraisals are momentarily). They will be much less lenient with deficiencies in the home than those appraisers of conventional borrowers.

For example, prior to 1978 lead-based paint was the norm. Most homes built before '78 contains lead-based paint. As science revealed the dangers of lead, it became illegal in that year. If you are pursuing an FHA loan and the house you want to buy was built in 1950, then the FHA inspector would take great exception should there be a room or two with flaking paint. The fix for this is relatively simple, all you do is paint those rooms, but should there be a disagreement between you (the buyer) and the seller over who should pay for the paint, it could spell deal breaker. My point is simply that your real estate agent should be well versed in what would be potential road blocks based on the type of financing you are pursuing and can advise you accordingly.

VA Loans:

VA loans are **V**eterans **A**dministration loans and are intended as a benefit for veterans of our armed forces. For those that have sacrificed and served this great country, please accept Melanie and I's sincere gratitude. That said; let's delve into what these loans mean. These loans operate very similarly to FHA loans, but you, having served in our armed forces and protecting my freedoms, deserve some extra privilege. Most VA programs allow you to not make a down payment. That's correct, zero, nada, nothin'. This is not to say that you won't be responsible for closing costs, however. That said, you will still need some cash. VA programs also follow very stringent regulations as far as the physical condition of the house upon inspection/appraisal as compared to their FHA cousin. They will want to make sure there are hand rails on the steps, GFI outlets in the bathroom(s) and kitchen, and, among other objectables, that pesky lead-based paint. Again, it is the job of a responsible agent to provide guidance and assistance relative to the form of financing you are seeking.

The Importance of Appraisals:

Regardless of what loan program you are pursuing, you will be hearing the word appraisal come up time and time again. Appraisals are ***<u>critical</u>*** (yep, that's bold, italics, and underlined due to its importance) to the successful purchase of real estate. Simply defined, let's offer an example:

You are over the moon in love with 123 Main Street. The list price is $110,000 and you offer $95,000. After some haggling back and forth you and the seller, with the assistance and guidance of your real estate agent, agree on a price of $100,000. Once you make your formal mortgage application, the bank will schedule the appraisal. Appraisers go through a stringent certification and licensing program to be able to expertly estimate the true value of a property. They are then hired by a bank to make sure that 123 Main Street is worth at least $100,000 in this example. As long as 123 Main Street appraises for at least $100,000 under this model, there are no worries. Conversely, if the appraiser comes back and says 123 Main Street is only worth, say, $97,000. Now, we have a problem. This means that the maximum the bank will loan you for this property is the $97K. This leaves a $3,000 gap in the original agreed upon price. There are four possible outcomes in this example:

1. You pony up the $3,000 in cash to shore up the difference.
2. The seller drops the agreed upon price by the same amount.
3. You, the buyer and them, the seller negotiate amounts from either side to satisfy the variance.
4. The deal is dead (play sad music in the background).

My point in this example is to illustrate that no one wins by overestimating the value of a property. At the end of the day, the lender holds a lot of power which needs to be respected because they are also holding a large amount of the risk. The lender is your friend, and take the advice of your real estate agent.

Timelines:

Regardless of what loan program you are pursuing, there will be stringent time lines. While some lenders can streamline these timeline estimates, traditionally, you are looking at about 45 days to close a conventional loan and about 60 days for FHA and VA loans. That said, your mortgage officer should be in constant communication with you as to what they need. They will ask for pay stubs, tax returns, gift letters (if applicable), etc. A gift letter is a letter from a friend or family member that has given you money to assist with the purchase of a home. The bank/loan originator requires this letter to ensure that the family member/friend is not requiring you to pay the money back. In addition to those items, there will be a host of documents they request. Typically, if they say they need it to be provided tomorrow, they actually needed it/them yesterday. It is up to you to get them produced in a timely manner. The original contract on the property will show an "on or before" settlement/closing date and any delays in providing items requested by your loan officer could put the whole deal in jeopardy. Simply put, if you actually want to buy 123 Main Street and you loan officer is asking you for something, anything, get it/them there quickly, efficiently, expeditiously… Just get them there!

Key chapter points:

1. Know your options.
2. Pick a loan option that's right for you.
3. Keep in contact with your loan officer (when they say they need it by tomorrow, they needed it yesterday).

"He who represents himself has a fool for a client"

-Abraham Lincoln

Four

IV. To hire or not to hire: The advantages of hiring a licensed Real Estate agent or Realtor®

Let me begin this chapter off by explaining what a Realtor *is*, and then I will follow up with what we are *not*. A licensed real estate agent does not necessarily mean that the individual is a Realtor. Once one passes the exam for the real estate license and files the appropriate paperwork with their state, they are a real estate agent. To become a Realtor, the agent has to be a member of the National Association of Realtors, for Melanie and I, the organization is the Pennsylvania Association of Realtors. Very frequently, people will interchange the terms real estate agent and Realtor. These memberships require annual dues. While Melanie and I are, in fact, Realtors, we will use the term "agent", just for consistency purposes. What does all this mean to you as the consumer? The major advantage for a real estate agent to become a Realtor is access to the Multiple Listing Service, or MLS, that is granted with these memberships (I will get into greater detail explaining the MLS in a moment). Another requirement for Realtors is that we must maintain training minimums which are not required simply by passing a real estate licensing test. The Associations listed above also have strict standards and bi-annual training for the code of ethics they adhere to and no-nonsense penalties for its members which fail to follow the code of ethics. This is a bunch of mumbo-jumbo which probably still leaves you asking, "What does this mean to me?"

Simply put, from the consumer (your) position, a great agent is an expert in their market. They are professional, accessible, knowledgeable, and patient. A great agent does more listening than talking in most cases. A great agent advises and gives suggestions but does so based on your needs. A great agent is a fierce advocate, an advisor, and a shrewd negotiator on their client's behalf. Above all, though, a great agent is honest and ethical in everything they do. In essence, it's someone that you would actually want to have a beer or a cup of coffee with after this process is complete. Someone that you can trust, yet enjoy their company.

With all that stated, let us discuss what the power of the MLS really means to you. The Multiple Listing Service allows access to every property listed for sale, through a broker. In this day and age (yes, I know I sound like your grandfather here), there are many websites that offer these listings, but nowhere offers real time listings that the MLS offers. This power unleashed, gives agents the ability to keep their thumb (and index, and middle, and ring, and pinky fingers) on the market. This capability gives their client (you) real time access to homes as they come on the market. Home buying can become very competitive. Properly priced homes will sell very quickly in most markets. It can be *extremely* frustrating for you to find the home of your dreams 3 days after it listed only to find out that someone beat you to it and the property is already under contract. As sales pitchy as this sounds, believe me, it happens! You will want the advantage of real time updates on your side as properties come on the market. The best part? While we suggest also browsing through homes, most agents can set you up with an auto-email that will notify you every time a house comes on the market that fits your parameters. All you have to do is call (or text… or smoke signal… carrier pigeon even) and let your agent know you want to walk through a home. We will get the appointment scheduled, get the necessary paperwork and phone calls made, and will meet you at the property.

The perception of the job of a real estate agent and what it actually is are very different. Let's admit it, we have all watched those TV shows where the client looks at three houses, chooses one, makes an offer, and, poof, the home of their dreams. The reality is that buying a home is complex series of negotiations. The most obvious one is making the offer. When you are constructing your offer, it is the agent's job to advise you on what the market is saying in regard to the home you are offering on. This does not mean the agent will say, "Offer <insert dollar amount here>". What it does mean is that if your inkling is to offer, let's say $100,000.00, the agent should advise whether your offer is competitive with the rest of the neighborhood relative to what has recently sold. On this same note, while many of the real estate apps and websites are great tools to find open houses and browse current listings, the "estimates" often provided are skewed. To no fault of the app, think about it – if a house is foreclosed and falling in on itself in a neighborhood that is typically a higher priced area, those numbers will significantly skew the estimate. An agent will be able to pull those numbers out (if applicable) and give you a fair market value to what the house can be worth (i.e. if you sold it tomorrow, would you get your money back?).

The other benefit, let's be honest, is face to face communication and physically having a real person to bounce ideas off of. For those of you who remember Jeeves… agents are like the Ask Jeeves (young'ens – Ask Jeeves was the "internet is brand new" version of Google). Most agents have connections and can refer inspections, loan originators, painters… you name it, and we usually know someone.

Most people think that agent's serve one purpose – obtaining access to homes that you want to look at. While that is very true, most of the work is done behind the scenes. Roughly 80% of the agents job is done from contract to closing.

Key chapter points:

1. An agent gives you real time access.
2. An agent is an expert in their market.
3. Refer back to the Honest Abe quote at the top of the chapter.

Five

"The only thing worse than being blind is having sight but no vision."

-Helen Keller

Worldwide Tour: Looking past the paint and carpet

We're finally looking at houses! You're excited. You saw pictures of a house online and it looks absolutely perfect. You book an appointment with your agent. Anxiously, you walk in and you are hit smack dab in the face with smell of cat pee… the rooms are smaller than the pictures led you to believe and the kitchen looks like they deep fried everything they ate. Did Bigfoot live here? There is more hair on the bathroom vanity than you have on your head (unless you're bald like my co-author). Not to mention the carpet is seafoam green and the bathroom tub is Barbie pink. Carpet in the bathroom? Why not.

Take a deep breath. Take a good hard look at the actual bones of the house. Is it something that after a little bit of blood, sweat and tears you could make into something truly beautiful? Walls are meant to be knocked down after all. (Well, most of them… we will get to that part later).   For those using any type of financing, there are a few specific things to pay close attention to. As we talk about the "guts" of the house later on, FHA (refer to Chapter 3) requires a few different things be "updated" in the house. The requirements are more to do with safety than aesthetics. Based upon your area, your agent will be able to walk you through what those requirements usually consist of.

Taking John's shirt example from Chapter 1 a step further, most people don't buy a shirt without knowing what pair of pants they own (or need to buy in the future) that will go with the shirt. That being said, you probably don't have the pants on when you're buying the shirt (hopefully you do have some pants on though at the store). You are just imagining it. However, unlike the shirt that can be exchanged or returned after purchasing it… it's not that easy to "return" a house. So that wants and needs list is very important in this chapter.

Before we delve completely into "what to look for", let's talk about what the seller of a home is obligated to inform you of. The seller has to put certain information pertaining to the home in writing. In the real estate world, we call this document a Seller's Disclosure. When selling a home, the seller is legally bound, in the state of Pennsylvania, to fill out a Seller's Disclosure. This may differ from state to state, but almost all states require the Seller's Disclosure. This form will tell you the last time any addition, correction, repair, alteration, or modification of the house was made within the scope of their knowledge. It will also, after signed by both parties, become an official document. When an offer is submitted, the Seller's Disclosure will also need to be initialed and signed off by you, the buyer, to acknowledge that you "accept the terms of the document" and what they're listing in the disclosure. If the seller reports that there was no water in the basement EVER during their time in the home, and then all of a sudden after a week of being in your new home the basement floods after a long rainstorm (you could, in essence, file a lawsuit for them not disclosing it in the disclosure). If the house was used as a rental, sold by a bank, or by an estate (estate = the owner has passed away and it is now being sold by either family or some other party), then technically, the seller does not know all, if any, issues, repairs, modifications, alterations, or corrections that happened in the home when they were not physically living there. Because they weren't physically occupying the property, they did not witness those things first hand. Anything that could have been reported to them from their tenants and/or family members was simply hear say. They may have knowledge of those things, but they still wouldn't be able to put that on paper. For situations like those, the seller would write "Seller Has Limited Knowledge" on the top of the form, and still sign off.

Quick disclaimer: no agent should ever proclaim to be an efficianto at determining the age of appliances, furnaces, hot water tanks, roof life... in fact, we can't. Under law, we are here to guide you through the home buying process as smoothly as possible, and help you make an informed purchase. We can absolutely do some research to try and find the answers to those questions. After submitting an offer on a home, depending on what you negotiated in the offer (more on that next chapter) you have a given number of days, per the contract, to do a home inspection. Most people opt for the home inspection, and some lenders even require it. The costs will vary and the options do as well, but it helps you understand the potential repairs that may need to be addressed. We will delve more into this in the following chapters.

Those that get this analogy will appreciate it... for those that don't, Google it. Remember Lincoln Logs? You couldn't start a house... a cabin... a fence for your fake ponies... without that one little notch log that interlocked all of the pieces, you were stuck with a whole bunch of nuthin'. For you millennials (and I'm one of you), it would be the equivalent of starting a LEGO garden without having the green plank. With that in mind, the first priority should be the structure and foundation of the home. Do you want to be "ooo'ed and aww'ed" over walking in? Of course! Everyone does! But real beauty in real estate, especially when on a budget, lies beneath.

Head to the basement of the home. When looking at the foundation (the structure in which the house is supported), you want to pay attention to the walls. Are they cracking? Do the cracks go straight down the wall and continue through the floor? Are the walls bowed in or out? Are they discolored? All of these things can create anxiety... most of which are not a big issue. For example, if the block walls in the basement have a few cracks, not a big deal. If the crack goes from the top of the wall into the middle of the floor in the basement – big deal. Bowing walls are also a cause of concern. Most houses, if they have walls that are bowed in, will require a structural engineer to ensure that the wall will not bow or shift anymore.

Are there stains on the walls or the flooring? Are they white or brown in color? Stains on the floor shows that some water may have been sitting on the basement floor for some period of time – it could be the result of a hot water tank issue, or a more significant issue. Usually white stains on the floor is from an interior water leak (pipe above, laundry machine, hot water tank), while brown stains are from water infiltration from the outside. Occasionally, white could also mean that it has been a persistent water leak and now it is developing mold. For stains on the walls, when it rains, water travels to any open area. The water tries to push through the brick, but the only thing making it through is the dirt that the water is pushing in. Hence why some walls have a rusty color to them. That is not a sign of a bad house. In fact, a lot of houses have that discoloration – it's normal. Now, if there is mold associated with discoloration, that's a different story. A good "clue" to any moisture in the basement, is if all of the guts (agent speak for furnace, hot water tank, etc.) are up on cinder blocks = not a good sign. Active water leakage is definitely different than just some infiltration during a rain storm or a leaky pipe.

If you see raised white spots (almost like yeast powder on a fresh loaf of bread) covered up with a black filmy substance… stay clear. More times than not, this is a sign of black mold. If you absolutely fall in love with the rest of the house, you will want to get a mold specialist in to see if it can be remediated.

While you're in the basement, look at the beams that are supporting the first floor (look up). Are they moldy? Are they crumbling? Are they soft to the touch? Ain't no one wants to be in their kitchen cooking and then fall into the basement. Those wooden beams support the foundation of the interior of the house. While looking at the beams, check out the pipes that run along those same boards. Do they have an active leak? A little condensation is normal, especially if the basement is cold, and the outside temp is warm, or if the house is vacant. The presence of an active water flow or a spot directly underneath one of the pipes may indicate a previous or active leak.

On a side note, if you're looking at houses that have been vacant for a while, and especially during the cold months, the seller (whether it's an individual or a bank) will more than likely winter-ize the house. That simply means that they will drain the water from all of the pipes (including the toilets) and shut off most of the utilities. Don't be alarmed.

This is actually a good thing. It prevents the pipes from freezing, and it mitigates the expenses that the seller pays during the months that the house is vacant. This is usually only a problem if you need to go pee (or worse, number 2!) in a house that you're looking at that has been winterized.

Venture over to the furnace. Most technicians will put a sticker on the furnace with the installation or last service date. Your home inspector will do the dirty work to make sure it works and is running efficiently, so no need to start pulling off the cover and checking the filter.

Next, look at the electric panel. Does it look like something created by Albert Einstein? (Then you can probably plan on replacing it). If they look like light switches that fell to their side (legit, picture a light switch, then picture it falling to its side) – you should be good. Circuit breakers are what you're hoping for.   A common item in older homes is knob and tube wiring. Knob and tube was used from the 1880 to the 1930's and looks very similar to one inch circular clips, holding wiring up in both the attic and the basement. If the home has knob and tube, it can be costly to replace, and in order to get financing, you may have to replace the knob and tube with a newer electrical panel and wiring. While it's negotiable for the seller to replace, most times, sellers know the knob and tube exist so get ready for negotiations. Also, in most states, the brand of electrical box named "Federal Pacific" will not be allowable for FHA or VA loans. A fuse box falls somewhere in the middle. Post 1930's but pre circuit breaker era. Fuses have the appearance of the bottom of a D battery. As opposed to the circuit breaker, than you can just flip the switch when it is tripped, the fuses you had to actually replace.

Now, those legs are made for walking. Head upstairs to the first floor. The aesthetics… carpet… paint? Feh-get-abut-em. Go directly outside. From the front or backyard, can you see the roof? If not… like, you know… try to walk back a few feet. No one can see a roof from standing right underneath an awning. Do the shingles appear to be "peeling up"? Are there spots where it appears as if shingles are missing? (Shingles are the little puzzle piece looking things that compose most roofs.) If so, it could be the product of one small wind storm, or faulty construction. Is the roof made of metal? Is the metal peeling up, or does it appear as if paint is chipping? While you're looking up, are there gutters on the house? Do they run from the roof to downspouts? Do those downspouts run to a place that won't go straight into the basement (downspouts that lead directly into the ground near the basement), or are they rerouted through a pipe that feeds out to the street? A big source of water problems in a basement, are just misplaced gutters and downspouts. If the downspout (the part of the gutter than runs from top to bottom of the house) just stops near the foundation – that could be a problem. They should typically 1) go underground or 2) have a curved pipe that runs a few feet away from the foundation.

Underneath an overhang of a house, there should be "soffit and fascia"; which are fancy words to describe the vinyl or aluminum pieces that allow the house to breath and prevent critters from crawling up the side of the house and getting in. There should be a piece every few feet that appears to have little holes in it. That's perfectly normal. Very similar to humans, houses sweat. Those little holes allow the house to breath.

Walk back inside. How do the windows look? Do they have peeling paint around the trim? Can they open? Do they lock? Are they cracked? Typically, this is an issue for FHA loan terms. If the windows have peeling paint (or anywhere on the exterior or interior of the home, actually), and the house was built before 1978, you will probably have to sand down the paint and encapsulate it (potentially by painting over the spot). The reason? Lead based paint was a common form of paint used prior to 1978. If there are spots where paint is peeling, the fear is that the lead based paint could be exposed. Going back to the windows, FHA also wants to make sure that in the case of a fire, that they are able to be opened.

Now, before you start analyzing the interior, as John had mentioned earlier, you have to answer one question – will this home be your forever home? Having that answer in the back of your mind helps you answer the "but could I live with it for 5 years?" question. If you tore out the seafoam green carpeting, removed the border wallpaper, painted the walls, and maybe took out a few walls to open up a few areas… would you love it? If the answer is no. Walk away. If the answer is maybe, head to the spot in the house that you spend the majority of your time. For me, I love to cook. So I would put a priority on standing in the kitchen and visualizing what I could do to make the house perfect for me. If you love family time and the living room is your spot, head there. After you've spent a few minutes in one area, trying to picture what you could do to make it yours, do a full loop around the house. Are the bedrooms the size you would like them to be? If not, can you live with them? Look up at the ceilings. Are there water marks from a bathroom or roof leak? While you're looking up, unless the house is brand new or freshly painted, most houses will have small hairline cracks near corners or door frames. Those are completely normal for an older (and sometimes newer) house. These cracks are not usually something to fret about. When a house is built, the wood usually has "moisture" in it. As it dries out, the wood expands (similar to a waistline during the holidays). The size and quantity of the cracks can be dependent upon the location of the home. In some areas of the country, with the change in weather, there could be more or less humidity, etc.

After you roam through the house, thinking about the little (or big) things you can do to update the home to your preferences, ask your agent, "If I did all of these things, and for some reason had to sell the house in a year, would I be able to get my money back?" Most agents would do a quick market assessment and give you the average of what the houses in that neighborhood are going for. Keep in mind, just because you put $10,000 into the kitchen of your dreams, does not mean that the person who would buy the house next, necessarily agrees with your investment.

If you're reading this book, you are probably also the same person who has been watching TV shows on house hunting and remodeling. I can't say I blame you… they can be addicting. Most of those shows usually don't show that they actually looked at 87 houses and not just three – to John's point of the crazy reality shows. Do not get discouraged if you don't find the house of your dreams in the first week. Or in the first month. This is a big purchase, and you never want to have regret over jumping on the first house that you looked at. That being said, when you know, you know. There have been many clients of mine that "weren't sure" and then lost the house because someone else swooped in and put in an offer before they did. While you want to be steadfast in your decision, you also don't want to drag your feet.

Okay, so you've decided on a house. You're nervous… excited… let's start the paperwork!

Key chapter points:

1. Carpet and paint – not make it or break it.
2. Keep your wants and needs list handy.
3. The bones (structure) of the house are most important.

Six

Offertime: Constructing an educated offer

Judge Judy is notorious for saying "the four corners of the contract". What exactly does that mean? When we construct a real estate offer, the only thing the seller/seller's agent can entertain is what we actually put on that paper. They can't guess what else we want from the house… they have no idea how much money you have in the bank for negotiation purposes… it is solely what we put on paper. Why does this matter? Let's delve in.

Two important terms. Offer – the contractual document before both parties sign off. Contract – a fully executed copy of the offer. One document, two parties – the buyer and the seller. The only thing preventing an offer from being a contract is the lack of the seller's signatures which will happen when they accept the offer.

While finding the perfect home that fits your needs and wants is the ultimate goal, the paperwork is the most crucial part to ensuring you have a seat at the closing table. The benefit to having an agent, in addition to what John described earlier, is to keep everyone that is involved cognizant of the timeline.

When you were looking at finances in Chapter 2 and 3, one thing we wanted to save for this chapter was "seller's assist". Seller's assist is a negotiation piece to have the seller pay a portion of your closing costs. A lender will run the numbers and tell you how much seller's assist you would be approved for… but what is it? Say you're looking at a $100,000 house, but you only have $3,000 saved up for closing costs. You could "ask" the seller (in the offer) to pay 3% sellers assist. This would have the seller contributing $3,000 (three percent of $100,000) towards your closing costs. What it actually means, is that the offer is $3,000 less; giving the seller $97,000 for their house. In essence, you are mortgaging in your closing costs.

The first step to the contract: figuring out how much you are actually willing to pay for the home. I call it "your tap-out point". Do you really love it to the point of full asking price? Or are you looking to do a lot of work, and would like to pay less to make up for some of the work that you will be doing to the home? By ethics, agents are required to produce every offer we get to the seller. There can be some method to the madness when figuring out the offer price. You will want to know the answers to the following: how long has the house been on the market? Have there been any other offers? What price did they pay for the home and when did they buy it? Did they do any updates? Is the house vacant? Is it a time of year that maybe the seller doesn't want the house to be vacant? For example, if a house has been on the market for a year (or more), and it is located in Erie, PA where we get more snow than the north pole, the seller may be more motivated to negotiating so they do not have to pay for heat and electric in the home over the course of the winter months. To the contrary, if the house has been on the market for two days, and while you were looking at the house, there were 4 other agents showing the property, you may not want to offer $10,000 less than the asking price, nor take a week deciding if it's the right house or not.

The tap-out point – how much do you love the house? Do you love it to get into a bidding war and pay more for the house than the list price? Do you only love it if you can get it for under the asking price? Your tap-out point isn't necessarily your initial offer. In the real estate world we call it "the best and final" offer. Meaning, it's love it and buy it, or lose it at that point.

After you establish your tap out point, consider how strong your offer is. Do you have money to put down, or are you utilizing seller's assist, as described previously? Did the bank require you to pay off a credit card before they will approve the mortgage application? Are you trying to close in the usual 6-8 weeks, or do you need to close later to fulfill the term of a lease agreement? Did you elect for every single inspection, or just the usual? All of these things weigh in when a seller is entertaining the offer(s) presented.

Contracts may differ from state to state, as do ones that you find online if you're trying to buy a house on your own. But in most cases, the first page of the contract is similar to a cover page. It will list the property, the buyers, the sellers, any agent involved, and the agent's real estate company (we call them Brokers). The next page will be the guts of the "offer". How much your offer is for, when you want to close by, when you're expecting to hear back from the seller in response to your offer (the norm is usually 2 days), and the part that we haven't talked much about yet – the earnest money deposit amount.

Earnest money is the equivalent of a security deposit on an apartment. In a previous life, I used to rent apartments to college students. I would describe the security deposit as "money that sits in the iCloud and you get it back when you move out". Don't judge me – it worked for students. In the home buying world, your earnest money is deposited and gets applied to your closing costs at closing. So what does it actually do? When paying a security deposit on an apartment, the intention is for you to have "buy in" or "partial ownership" to keep the apartment intact, with fear of losing that money when you move out. It also acts as leverage for prompt payment of rent allowing the landlord to mitigate the damage financially to themselves if you just up and leave. They would be able to use that security deposit to recover at least one month's rent. In real estate, the earnest money deposit is your way of saying to the seller, "Mr. Seller, I'm going to do everything within my power to follow the timeline of the contract, and keep my finances in order until I get the keys at the closing table". In most cases, the amount of the earnest money deposit is proportionate to the price of the home. It could be $2,000 for a $80,000 home and $10,000 for a $250,000 home. At the end of the day, the amount of the deposit is negotiable. It just has to be significant enough that you wouldn't want to jeopardize losing that money.

Does this mean you have to have that money in the bank when submitting an offer? Yes. In the simplest terms, while the contract is a contract by definition, the earnest money deposit makes it official. I know what you're thinking. But if something comes back in the home inspection that I no longer want the house, do I get the earnest money deposit back? Or what if I lose my job, and that was out of my control? Yes. You would receive the deposit back. However, if you just quit your job for no good reason, there may be a case that the seller would have to keep the deposit. In essence, the earnest money compensates the seller for the amount of time that the house was off the market, when they could have potentially sold it to someone else. We will get into the home inspection process and earnest money deposit in the next chapter.

So now, you have your tap out point, you know how much money you need to present with the offer… now what? The next few pages of the contract will be relevant to your financing. The check box that is very important for you or your agent to check mark is "contingent upon mortgage". Unless you're pulling cash out from underneath your mattress… then that box would be irrelevant. That box tells the seller's that if for some reason, your mortgage application doesn't go through, you can walk away with your earnest money deposit. Unless, you did something silly like open a new Kohl's account to save 20% on a $15.00 purchase. I know John mentioned it in the previous chapter's, but during this time from submitting an offer to closing, you do NOT want to open any new credit lines or have any hits on your credit. The only acceptable "new bills" are the utilities for the new home, which you won't be transferring into your name until closer to closing.

Also in this section of the contract, you or your agent, will list the amount of your down-payment, your mortgage amount, your maximum interest rate, the term of your loan – all of the stuff that is relevant to your mortgage. For example, if you were quoted at a 4% interest rate, and have a maximum interest rate listed on the contract of 8%, and then when you apply for the mortgage, the interest rates sky rocket to 10%, you could walk away from the deal. Very seldom does this happen, but if the housing market takes a dive, it's nice to have that little caveat in there. Refer to the real estate crash of 2008, not mentioned in this book.

Is the pre-approval the same as a mortgage application? As John described it, not even close. The pre-approval is the banks way of saying "we think you can afford this much of a house, based upon your income and your debt to income (how much of your income goes to bills and credit lines)?" In most cases, the contract stipulates that within 7 days of the offer, you have to apply for the mortgage. To do so, you would go back to the mortgage originator or bank that issued you the pre-approval, and they would walk you through what documents they need to get that started.

Does having a pre-approval from one bank preclude you from going to multiple banks to shop around rates? Not at all. In most areas, there are actual mortgage companies that will do that shopping around for you. Many banks offer roughly the same interest rates, but some may have different programs for first time home buyers. It is very important though that you do this BEFORE submitting an offer. Your lender of choice will be listed on the offer and the pre-approval letter needs to be attached to the offer.

The next part is equally important as the previous timelines. Your home inspections. We'll get into more detail about this in the next chapter, but you will be picking from a cornucopia of different types of inspections. The two most important are home and pest. Most FHA and VA loans require both of these inspections to be done. The others inspections, while they vary through state, would consist of land and property lines, water and sewage testing, and radon and other harmful gas/chemical testing. In most cases, if the water and sewer are run by the municipality (otherwise known as public water and public sewer) then you do not need the water and sewer tests. If the property has a well and/or septic tank, you will probably want to opt in for those inspections to make sure everything is working appropriately. Most boundary and property information could be obtained at the local courthouse without paying for an inspection and most home buyers don't have a need for these inspections. As for the radon and other gas/chemical testing, it is usually geographically specific. Most agents would be able to advise you based upon the property, which inspections related to gas and chemicals would make sense for that specific property. If you are doing this on your own, make sure to do some research on what is relevant to your area.

Scattered through the rest of the contract puts the "odds and ends" on paper. Is the house a historical landmark that precludes you from tearing down any walls? Meaning, did George Washington ever live in the house? Is it in a flood plain? Do you have diamonds, natural gas and gold underneath the surface in your backyard? Well, wouldn't that be nice.

While contracts (as mentioned before) may differ from state to state; the contracts that we are familiar with will list the responsibilities of the seller in the last few pages. Such as, if there is any loss or damage to the property, the sellers are responsible and cannot apply your earnest money deposit to recoup that loss/damage; being diligent regarding timelines and providing the proper documentation requested, and by maintaining the property in its current condition and holding home insurance in their name until the time of closing. The seller's disclosure, mentioned in the previous chapter, becomes an addendum to the contract. Meaning "part" of the contract. By initialing all of the pages of the seller's disclosure, you're acknowledging that you read and accept the document and its contents.

There are only a few parts in contract talking about the items in the home. In these sections, items that aren't attached to the structure of the home should be listed for inclusion or exclusion. For example, light fixtures. If it is not specifically indicated in the contract that you would like to "exclude" those items from the purchase, the seller has to keep them intact. Appliances however, if you would like to keep them, would be listed under the "included" section. Items usually listed in the "included" section are typically kitchen appliances, washer and dryers, and backyard decor (ie. hot tubs, pools, playgrounds, occasionally a lawn mower, etc). It is also in this section that you have to take in to account your offer price. If you really want the house, and you know you have a relatively "weak" offer (full seller's assist and lower than asking price offer), you may have to be willing to forego the "extra items" during negotiations. Everything listed in the offer is up for negotiation. For example, if the seller doesn't love your offer price, and knows that you really want the fridge, they may bump up the price of their counter and include the fridge. I am very much a believer of asking for everything you want, then using those pieces to negotiate the perfect deal. These "extra" items are listed separately so as to not "add value" to the offer price. For example, if you're including the refrigerator, the appraiser is not going to take into account the value of the fridge when it comes to giving a value of the home.

One thing to keep in mind, some sellers when listing their home, include a home warranty. A home warranty, in essence, is similar to health insurance for your house. If something covered by the warranty goes wrong within the first year post purchase, you can call the home warranty company, and they'll send one of their contracted plumbers, HVAC techs, electricians, etc. over to fix the problem. Some home warranties even include appliances that were currently in the home. There is a small co-pay that you would then be responsible for, but if you're looking at a $1,000 plumbing job and you are responsible for only $50 of it… a worthy investment. Just because a seller isn't including a home warranty, doesn't mean you can't ask for one or purchase your own. Just remember, the "stronger" the offer, the more likely it will be accepted. The more you ask for, to the point from before, weakens the offer.

After everything is filled out, you will initial all of the pages and sign the last page. If you're doing this on your own, you will want to keep a copy of the offer for you, and get one to the seller or the seller's agent. In a case where you are representing yourself, but the seller has an agent, it would go to the agent. In a case where both parties have an agent you sign on the lines and let them do the rest.

Keep in mind; if you are really low balling a property (trying to get the house for significantly less than asking price) some sellers and agents will entertain the idea of a verbal offer. By no means does this replace an actual offer in writing, but if you want to gauge if the other party will even entertain the price you're thinking about, it saves everyone time by attempting to go this route first. It should be noted though that if there's another offer that is being presented in writing that is coming in at the same time as your verbal offer, the seller's agent has no obligation to present your verbal offer to the sellers.

So now what? Everything is signed. Your agent submitted the paperwork to the other agent … Now. You. Wait.

Within one or two days, the seller's will review the offer. They have the ability to counter it with any type of changes they choose. Maybe they want to keep the fridge that you're asking for, or maybe it's a higher price point. They will submit those changes in writing to your agent. You and your agent will discuss and then resubmit a counter offer to their counter. Typically, if both agents are good communicators, and as long as there aren't multiple offers coming in on the property, a deal should be reached within a week.

What happens if the sellers are not willing to negotiate and counter at the asking price of the house? This is where you have to go back to the notion of the "tap-out" point. If you're changing your mind regarding how much you're willing to pay, maybe schedule a second (or third) showing at the home. Occasionally being back in the home will help solidify your gut feeling.

Key chapter points:

1. Pay close attention to timelines and details.
2. Read the contract.

Seven

Annnd accepted: A brief celebration, but, wait, there is more work to be done.

Your agent calls you a few days later and says "the other agent is meeting with their seller tonight, so I should know something". What do you do? You get even more anxious. What if they don't accept? What if you have to start this process all over again? What if? You carry your phone anxiously around in your hands, just to not miss the call. Phone rings. You pick up. ANNNDDD ACCEPTED! They accepted your offer! You're excited. Your agent is excited for you. You just cleared one of the biggest hurdles in buying a home! After a brief period of "yay's" and "I'm so happy for you", the real work has to begin. A word of advice – this is not the time to post anything to social media. Tell a few close family and friends, but if something should fall through, nothing is harder than getting back into the saddle of house hunting and feeling defeated. There is still a long way to go before the keys are slid across the table.

First, if you elected to give the seller the earnest money deposit after they accepted the offer, you will need to get a check to your agent as soon as possible. If you fail to do so, it could jeopardize getting the house by voiding the contract, and subjects you to potential legal problems. If you gave the deposit at the time of drafting the offer, you don't have to worry about this step.

There are three specific timelines to adhere to that your agent will keep you on track with. The first? The mortgage application. We touched on it briefly earlier, but you now have to physically start the paperwork for the mortgage. They will ask you for previous year's tax returns, proof of employment, all kinds of stuff. The quicker that you get the application and corresponding documents to the loan originator, the better. They cannot start the "underwriting" process until all of the documents they are requesting have been turned in. What is underwriting? Not to be confused with an "undertaker", "underwriting" is the process of the bank going through all of the nitty gritty of your past. All of your credit lines, your employment history… they're in essence making sure they want to be married to you for the next thirty years with the loan. A step in the underwriting process is the appraisal. Some people confuse inspection and appraisal, which is easy to do. The inspection is a third party's observations and beliefs of the property. We will get into this in the next paragraph. The appraisal is the bank's "contractor" valuing the house that you agree to put as collateral for the mortgage. Example: if you're paying $80,000 for a home and you're trying to get a loan for $75,000, the bank wants to be sure that if you don't make a payment and they need to take the home back (i.e. Foreclose on the home) that they could resell it and make their money back. So what happens if the bank doesn't think that the house is worth what you're paying for the home? This is a tricky situation. First item to look at – are you asking for sellers assist? If so, it could be one of the first things to "have to go" on the contract. Occasionally, when you're financing in your closing costs, the seller will ask for a higher price. If that higher price (in order to allow for sellers assist) puts you above the appraisal, the seller will more than likely nix the sellers assist.

However, if there is no sellers assist or even on occasions where there is, a lower appraisal usually happens when there aren't many houses similar to the one that you are buying in the same area. There are two options here. The first is a second appraisal. 9 times out of 10 if the appraisal comes in significantly different than the offer price, a second appraisal would be a waste of money. The second option is to go back to the negotiation table. If the house can't appraise at what the sellers were asking for the home, then it is likely that the seller would have trouble selling it to anyone at that price with any type of financing. So even if your deal falls apart, they would re-list the property and hope that someone came in with a cash offer. Good news for you – this usually drops the price of the home to the appraisal price. I know what you're thinking. Does that mean that if it appraises higher that they can ask for more money? Good question. No. It just means that you did a great job at negotiating and picking a great house for your hard earned money.

While the bank does its' thing with underwriting, you still have two more deadlines to stick to. After the offer is accepted, you have work to do! If negotiated in the contract, you have a set amount of time to get an inspection. While these dates can vary, it will depend on what you and your agent decided to write into the contract. The norm is usually 10 to 20 days from the time of the accepted offer. This deadline is applicable to any and all inspections you requested in your offer. Typically, there are different inspectors for all of the different inspections; however, it doesn't hurt asking if the inspector does home and pest, or any of the other ones you selected. Your agent can typically suggest a few different inspectors that they would recommend, but you are absolutely allowed to call around to different places, look at different reviews online, and do some price comparisons. One thing to keep in mind, especially during the spring and summer (up north especially), inspectors are very busy. It's very important to call within a few days of the offer being accepted to get the inspection booked.

It's the day of the home inspection. Most buyers attend the inspection, but they are not required to. During the inspection, the home inspector may say things like "you probably have about X number of years left on the roof". They will not include those statements in the report, because there's no science, just experience, as basis to those statements. But for what it's worth, those are helpful little nuggets to keep in mind. After the inspection is complete (usually about three hours, depending upon the size of the house), the inspector will take their notes and within a few days, send you and your agent a copy of the home inspection. At that time, you and your agent will sit down and fill out what we call, a "Reply to Inspection", or as my co-author jokes about all the time, "RTI as they say in the biz". At this time, you will discuss the things that the bank may require to be fixed and the other things that you just personally want to see done. For example, the bank wants to know that the house isn't going to burn down after they give you the mortgage, that it's structurally sound, and that the liability is minimal. The items that they often require: no peeling paint if the house was built before 1978 (lead based paint), that the electric is up to date, and that the structure of the home is solid.

After the "Reply to Inspection" is complete, your agent then sends it off to the seller's agent. At that time, the clock starts ticking. The seller typically has five days to respond back to what they would be willing to either physically do, or pay a contractor to do. After they respond **(and again, each state varies with timelines, as well as each contract – depending upon what was negotiated),** you have two days to keep going back and forth. So what happens if you can't get to an agreement? If after a few counters to the Reply to Inspection, you're not feeling satisfied, you have the ability to walk away from the purchase with your earnest money deposit in hand. In most cases though, an agreement can be reached regarding the repairs.

The third timeline is the overall timeline. As discussed, in most cases, on the second page of the contract it lists the "Settlement Date". In real estate terms, it just really means "the day that the house can actually be yours". Barring any issues, it typically takes a bank 4-6 weeks to complete the underwriting process, so most closings happen 6 to 8 weeks after the offer is accepted. Some lenders can process the paperwork quicker, even within two weeks, but the majority of companies are still at the more traditional window of 6-8 weeks. During that time period, the inspections, the mortgage documents, everything needs to be completed. Also during that time, you will have to reach out to a title company (also called a settlement company) who will start preparing the title searches and deed preparation. The deed = the document saying you have rights to the house. The title searches? To make sure no one else has rights to the house, and that there aren't any past due liens (liens = bills = unpaid mortgages, construction loans, etc.) on the property. It is commonly referred to as "a clean title", which simply means you (and the bank) will be the only ones with rights to the property. Some people will choose to call an attorney (who can also do real estate closings) instead of a title company.

As the Settlement Date gets closer, you will receive two very important items. The closing disclosure and the clear to close. The clear to close isn't represented by a specific media, it will more than likely come via phone call or email from the settlement office or the loan originator. The clear to close is the equivalent of seeing the finish line while running a race. You're not there yet, but you can see it. After you receive that news, you will then set up a time with the settlement office for the closing. Hang in there! The keys are almost in your hand! Once closing is booked, 72 hours or before, you will receive a closing disclosure from the settlement (or attorney's) office. This little paper may make your tummy turn a little bit. It will have listed where every cent of your money is going. Every. Single. Penny. That's a lot of pennies.

While regulations and laws change all the time, it's currently a law that you cannot close before the 72 hour mark of receiving the closing disclosure. This is to ensure two things. One, that there aren't any mistakes regarding the breakdown of expenses and two, that you have ample time to get a check with the amount of money you still owe to buy the home. While we would love to all walk around with briefcases of cash, a cashier's check will be required the day of closing with the final amount due. You typically have a ball park idea of what this amount will be. If you anticipate 6-8% of the purchase price in closing costs (the 3.5% down payment for an FHA loan and a random assortment of the 2.5% of "other stuff" like water bill proration, tax proration, filing fees, settlement fees), and you know that you gave an earnest money deposit of $1,000, the ball park figure would be something like this: $100,000 home x .06% for closing costs = $6,000. $6,000 – the earnest money deposit of $1,000 = $5,000. In the case of seller's assist, this is where the seller's assist would be applied. $6,000 - $1,000 earnest money deposit – the amount in seller's assist = "cash to close".

It is **VERY** important to reiterate here, that **FOR NO REASON**, should you open up any new credit lines, get a new vehicle, lend anyone money… anything that could hurt your credit or the amount you have in your bank account. The only thing you can and should do pertains to the utility bills of your future home.

During the final week, you will want to call the utility companies (gas and electric) to transfer service into your name. It's important that you do this before the closing day to avoid shut off/start up fees. If you call to "transfer" they will simply transfer those utilities into your name, as opposed to canceling service from the seller's and creating an entire process for you to regain service. The settlement office will handle the water and sewer if applicable.

One. Last. Step. Literally. A final walk through. A day or two before closing, you and your agent will want to schedule a final walk through of the home. This is to prevent any "ummm, they were supposed to keep the fridge here" type of moments. The contract also stipulates that the house must be left in "broom clean" condition. That simply means all personal belongings must be removed, and it should have at least been lightly cleaned. In some cases, if you are taking the property in "as is" condition, the removal of belongings and the "broom clean" condition state, may not apply. Now you've reached it: Closing Eve. You are almost there. One. More. Sleep.

Key chapter points:

1. Do not open any new credit lines or do anything to effect the amount of money you have saved up for closing costs.
2. Inspections dates and requests are CRUCIAL to your deposit.
3. Know. Your. Dates.

Eight

Closers: What it truly means when the keys are slid across the table

HAPPY CLOSING DAY! That was a quickest, longest, emotional high 6-8 weeks! With your cashier's check in hand, your driver's license (because they'll need to make a copy of it at closing to make sure it's you!) and a smile on your face and a butterfly the size of T-Rex in your tummy, you walk into the closing office. This location can be an attorney's office or a settlement agency. Your agent will usually meet you there to ensure everything goes smoothly. They will have all of the paperwork you have signed and accumulated over the last few months to make sure everything nothing gets missed.

The settlement agent will walk you through every single document. You will initial and sign your name a lot. You'll pretend to read the papers, but your mind will be racing. You are finally going to be a home owner! In some cases, the buyers and sellers are in the same room during closings. In other cases, they are in different rooms. Occasionally, one party will pre-sign their documentation (mostly for the case of "out of town" owners). There is no right or wrong way; as long as someone has the one item that you've been waiting for – the keys!

The key is finally slid across the table to you, the settlement agent stands up to shake your hand, and you… you my friend, are finally a homeowner! After you wipe your sweaty, clammy, nervous hands on your pants, you may do whatever you want. Go roll around on the carpet in the house, start moving stuff in, or go celebrate with friends. Either way, you have finally made it to closing day!

Key chapter points:

1. Try to pay attention to what the settlement agent is saying.
2. Wear pants – to wipe your sweaty hands on.
3. You. Are. So. Close.

Nine

Welcome home: The white picket fence

As you finally turn your new house into a home; whether that encompasses a huge renovation or simply renting a moving truck… you can finally take a deep breath and be proud of what you just accomplished. Home ownership is one of the pillars of success in this life, and you did what you set out to do. Whether the home you just purchased is a stepping stone, or your forever home, always renovate with the intention to sell. I know, I know! The furthest thing from your mind right now is going through the process of house hunting again! However, keep these things in mind while making the finishing touches:

Upgrading the guts of the house is costly… but a necessity. If re-selling the house in one year or a hundred years, a potential buyer is going to want to see that the electrical box, the hot water tank, the furnace, all of the things that make the house "run" are updated. If you spend $10,000 on a new electrical system, you will see very little of that back when you go to sell the house; however, it will make the home more marketable.

On the same lines, a roof is essential to keeping the elements of nature out. A faulty, leaky roof decreases the value of the home significantly. On the same note, if you spend $10,000 on a new roof, it is unlikely that you will see that $10,000 come back in the form of an increased purchase price. But, again, a necessity.

At the current time, the highest ROI (return on investment) items are: new garage doors, new entry doors, minor kitchen and bathroom remodels, and new siding (or polishing up the "curb appeal"). By ROI, all we mean is if you spend $3,000 on a new garage door, or $15,000 on a "minor" kitchen remodel, you will most likely be able to see that return when you resell the house.

Obviously, things like location, other houses on the market, and current market conditions weigh heavily on the above. You can put a new kitchen in a property, but if the surrounding properties are the equivalent of cardboard boxes, it would be tough to see the ROI.

Probably one of the scariest things about owning a home are the costs associated with it. No longer can you call a landlord if the furnace stops working, or if a pipe is leaking. So pay special attention to having some cash in a savings account, that mythical creature from before, for those unexpected joys of home ownership.

Well, there you have it. You officially are a home owner. Good luck, God speed, and don't forget – when in doubt, when not in doubt, call one of us and we can walk you through it!

Key chapter points:

1. This house is **YOURS**. In sickness, and in health… all yours!
2. Keep the future in mind when doing any updates.
3. Save, save, save for unexpected maintenance items.

About the Authors

John Beuchert:

John, born and raised in Erie, PA, started his broad resume in 1989 at the ripe old age of 13 sprinting through his newspaper route attempting to make it back to school in time for basketball practice. Always 5 minutes late, the wind sprints that followed put him in the best shape of his life. A 1993 graduate of Cathedral Preparatory School took him to Penn State University where he graduated in 1996 with a degree in Administration of Justice. Through these years, John has worked an array of jobs… He has experience in cemetery maintenance, residential landscaping, retail loss prevention, private security, and tending bar (go ahead and ask him to make your favorite drink!).

Following his time at Penn State, John has had an ongoing 20-year career in the criminal justice field. He has worked both as a corrections and police officer. He credits both his time inside "the gate" and on the street for honing his ability to calm people under stressful situations.

John then decided to take his education and experience to transition into the world of real estate. He obtained his Pennsylvania real estate license and has been assisting home buyers and sellers with the same vigor that the citizens he serves enjoy.

In his downtime, John enjoys watching his two daughters competing (much better than he did) in sports. He spends time reading, writing, and enjoying the great doors with a fishing pole in his hand. Professionally, John takes pride in providing the greatest service available to his clients.

Melanie Brewer:

Melanie began her working career salting pork bellies to later be turned into bacon at a local meat market at age 12. Her work ethic and aspirations led her to attend the prestigious Collegiate Academy in her native Erie, PA; graduating in 2004. She graduated from Penn State University with a double major in International Business and Management and double minors in Political Science and Biology; graduating in 2008. Her initial career path while in college was to train Shamu. This afforded her the opportunity to study abroad in Costa Rica and chase mating turtles throughout Presque Isle, but once realizing that there are only so many Shamus, she redirected her trajectory towards business and politics.

College workload did not stop her from adding to her resume. During this time, she worked as a security guard at a local hospital and managed a regional grocery store.

Her passion for politics, passed on from her father, took her to serve in several roles on the local, state and national levels. She has managed campaigns, raised funds, consulted and attended every pot luck dinner from here to oblivion supporting her candidate. These candidates have included local township supervisors, city mayors, local judges, state senators, and US Congressmen.

Melanie's love of politics was trumped by her love of her family when she decided to stay local as opposed to pursuing opportunities in Washington D.C. She then accepted an opportunity to manage senior and student housing communities for a local development company, where she was responsible for the leasing and marketing, as well as over-seeing daily operations for over 1500 apartments. It was here that she fell in love with real estate and the opportunity to assist and advocate for people buying and selling their homes. Melanie became a licensed agent and Realtor in 2012, and has helped over 100 families find or sell their home. In 2018, still loving real estate, she wanted a change in her "day job" and accepted a position with a home health care company, where she manages over 125 employees, and together, they provide nursing care to over 100 children in the Erie County area.

In her downtime, she enjoys brainstorming business ideas, serving on local boards, and traveling. Professionally, Melanie most enjoys seeing a project all the way through to its end goal.

Appendix

Be patient with your agent. The most frustrating part of our jobs - lock boxes and light switches.

If your bladder or tummy calls while looking at houses, flush the toilet first to make sure the water is on.

While everything is negotiable, the cars in the driveway are usually not.

Most importantly – have fun, laugh a lot, and enjoy the process!